Table of Contents

LET JUSTICE
ROLL ON LIKE A RIVER

Please God

By

C.O. Stephens

Let Justice Roll On Like A River
Publication © 2020 Mbokodo Publishers
Text © 2020 CO Stephens
ISBN-13: 978-1-990919-63-3 (Paperback)
ISBN-13: 978-1-990919-64-0 (PDF)
ISBN-13: 978-1-990919-65-7 (eBook)[1]
Publisher: M.R. Mbokodo
Proofreading: CO Stephens
Cover Design: M.R. Mbokodo
Published by

---

1. http://www.mbokodopublishers.eshop.co.za/

Typeset in 10/12 Adobe Garamond Pro by Mbokodo Publishers
Printed by Mbokodo Publishers 1 2 3 4 5 1 2
mbokodopublishers@gmail.com

This term has been used so much, and in so many ways, that it becomes a bit ambiguous.

In English, there is a clear distinction between the words "evangelical" and "Protestant". However, in other languages like Portuguese, the word to translate "Protestant" is "Evangelico". Martin Luther, to the Portuguese-speaker, was an "Evangelico". Whereas in English, he was a "Protestant", perhaps the most prominent figure in the Protestant Reformation.

For the purposes of this booklet, we just have to admit that there is some ambiguity in the word.

Broadly speaking, the word "evangelical" is often used to refer to non-mainline churches. That is, to the church denominations from Baptist to Mennonite to Pentecostal, that emerged at the "radical" end of the spectrum during the Reformation. In Britain, these came to be called "non-conformist" because the mainline or Anglican church was "conformist".

The Protestant church emerged during the Reformation – for example *Lutheran* in Germany, *Reformed* Church in Holland and Scotland (where it was called *Presbyterian*) and *Anglican* in England (i.e. the Church of England founded by Henry VIII and championed by his daughter Elizabeth I and her nephew who succeeded her and authorized the King James version of the English Bible).

Breaking away from the hegemony of Rome was tumultuous, and is one explanation for the migration of whites to the Cape in South Africa. Basically, the conflict in Europe between Roman Catholics and Protestants got very nasty. This played out differently in different countries. Sometimes it was a case of just crossing the English Channel to Holland, like William Tyndale did. The Bibles that he translated into English and then printed in Holland were then smuggled back across the Channel into England, by Protestant merchants. This further loosened the hegemony of Rome in England, until Henry VIII finally relented. (Some would say that he relented for his own personal reasons, not for theological ones.) The king pardoned Tyndale and invited him to return home. But alas. The Counter-Reformation managed to capture him, strangle him and burn his body at the stake, while still in Europe.

Another scenario was that of persecuted Protestants migrating to the new colonies which were opening up in America and South Africa. The Huguenots, for example, fled from France under persecution, into Switzerland, then to Holland, where they embarked to South Africa en masse.

John Calvin started his protest in Paris. He was hugely influential, perhaps second to Martin Luther in Germany. He ended up in Geneva, in a mixed church and state role. Because the moderate Reformers, from which we have inherited the "mainline churches" still believed in a strong connection between church and state. The Lutheran church is therefore now the State Church in Germany. And for centuries until 1994, the Dutch Reformed Church (DRC) effectively became the State Church in South Africa. This of course switched on and off again, depending on whether the Dutch or the English were holding supremacy of the high seas. Capetown was a strategic port in that see-saw of predominance, so the Anglican church was at times, and by some, seen as the "official" church. And thus the Anglican archbishop is regarded by many as the senior churchman in the country.

The ambiguity of the word "evangelical" can be tracked through this period. Because most "evangelicals" would claim the likes of Martin Luther, John Calvin and William Tyndale as their own. In Britain, the Calvinists were Presbyterians – thus "non-conformists", whereas in Holland and South Africa, they were the predominant or mainline denomination.

But the word "evangelical" would also encompass the "radical Reformers" whose views varied, but essentially harmonized on the separation of church and state. The Anabaptists were among these – because re-baptizing members as adults was symbolic of trashing the old church altogether, along with infant baptism, which continued to be practiced by moderate Reformers like Lutherans.

Mennonites are named after Menno Simmons of Holland. To Mennonites, salvation does not come from either the sacraments (Catholic view) or from conversion (i.e. justification by faith, championed by Luther), but rather from *community*. Within a separate enclave of Christians who live and work together, separated from the broader society, your salvation comes to you.

This is related to the two different notions of "parish churches" and "member churches". The Catholic hierarchy is based at the Vatican, which itself is a State. Its work across the world is divided into "parishes". A priest is basically responsible for everyone in that geographical area, not just for those who profess to be Catholic. This view continues among the moderate reformers, the mainline churches. This sense of responsibility may be rejected by some in the community, but it is there.

Whereas to Baptists, Mennonites, Congregationalists, Pentecostals and Africa-initiated churches like Zion Christian Church, pastors are responsible for their "flocks". At least first and foremost. Not to the exclusion of those outside the fold, but when you cross that boundary, it is "out"reach.

This could explain why evangelicals and Pentecostals have tended not to "engage the powers" in terms of advocacy and lobbying? They see this as somehow outside their jurisdiction, as if prevailing policies and practices did not affect their members! This "complacency" is ill-conceived.

The ambiguity of the word "evangelical" cannot be corrected. It is as it is. I describe myself as a "charismatic evangelical Catholic". In other words, as an "Angli-Bapti-Costal".

2.1 Was St Francis an early evangelical?

I have a lot of time for the "poverello". He somehow recognized the need for change, but at the same time he understood that the Roman church was gridlocked into its State role, for the time being. The emergence of nation-states like Germany, England and France was not yet on the horizon. Rome still reigned supreme. So he rather set a personal example that challenged the status quo. He brought Refreshment, not Reformation.

The followers of St. Francis were divided – some wanted to simply follow his example, others wanted to "go for it" and rock the boat. It is interesting to note that these tendencies among some Franciscans tended to be outside of Italy, on the peripheries, geographically speaking. For example, in northern Europe. In due course, this is of course where the challenge to Rome's hegemony would come from.

I also have a lot of time for St Augustine. Not just because he was an African, like many of the early church fathers were. (And even one of the Twelve Disciples: Bar-Ptolemy.)

Perhaps the question is really, can Roman Catholics be "evangelicals" too? My sense is, why not? Martin Luther was a Catholic priest, who came to the defining criteria of Protestantism – justification by faith – by studying the Scriptures. This can happen time and again, to anyone.

We need to find one another again. One of the ways to do so is to recognize our different strengths and to learn from one another. To me, one of the greatest strengths of the Roman church hierarchy is the presence of the Catholic Commission of Justice and Peace, where ever you go. Because the Vatican is a State, it constitutes this entity in each country to "engage the powers".

Is it any surprise then, that the investigation into "State Capture" in South Africa, which started when Thuli Madonsela was our Public

Protector, was triggered by a complaint form completed and signed by father Stanislaus Mayibe, a Dominican priest, from the CCJP? Madonsela concluded that a judicial inquiry should be set up, and that led to the work of the Zondo Commission.

2.2 Morning stars of the Reformation

Usually this title of "morning star" is attributed to John Wycliffe, at Oxford. He was the first to complete an English translation of the Bible. And he was a very outspoken cleric, although he can be critiqued for hypocrisy (like most of us can be).

My reason in mentioning him is that his probing into societal issues eventually led to a Peasants' Revolt. This happened in 1381, and it was both unprecedented and a portent. The three leaders of the rebellion were Jack Straw, Wat Tyler and a country priest called John Ball. His stirring sermon to the rebels is summarized by Benson Bobrick in his book <u>Wide as the Waters</u>, and what it led to:

"He urged his listeners to remember that all men had been created equal, and that manorial serfdom was an evil creation devised by the rich and powerful purely to benefit themselves. For twenty years Ball had been preaching a kind of communism throughout the north of England, before he carried his message to London and its suburbs...

"The rebels invaded London, destroyed Marshalsea prison, gutted Lambeth Palace, ransacked the estate of John of Gaunt, and beheaded numerous victims is spasms of random violence in Cheapside. A number of high officials took refuge in the Tower, which also served as the king's headquarters in the rebellion's last turbulent days...

"Many mansions throughout the city, in Westminster, Highbury, and elsewhere, were set ablaze, and "the young king Richard, from a high turret window, watched the conflagrations reddening the sky...

"The king agreed to meet and negotiate with the rebel leaders at Mile End, where he affected wholesale concessions – nothing less than the complete abolition of serfdom...

"The exulting peasants then poured back into town through Aldgate. But the king and his advisors did not proceed in good faith. "If they had'" remarked G.M. Trevelyan, "they would have haggled more over the terms.

They regarded it only as a means of freeing themselves from the present situation, as King John had regarded Magna Carta, and as Charles I later regarded the Petition of Right."

"Although thousands of rebels, trusting to the king's concessions, had left London, those that remained made other demands – for the disendowment of the Church (with a redistribution of its wealth), abolition of the game laws, free use of the woods, and so on. This led to a final confrontation between them and the king's men. In the market square of Smithfield outside London, the mayor of London, flanking King Richard, got into an altercation with Wat Tyler and stabbed him to death.

"In the end, the privileges which had been wrung from the king by the rebels were revoked, hundreds were tried and executed as traitors, and when challenged about his promises at Mile End, the king replied: "villeins ye are and villeins ye shall remain."

For over a decade by this time, John Wycliffe has been raising impertinent questions in his dual role as priest and professor. He had got himself into academic hot water more than once, and was regarded as a maverick. However, not even Wycliffe could foresee how empowering the poor and "unleashing the laity" would spill over into politics.

Jan Hus was from Bohemia – what is now the Czech Republic. He had heard about Wycliffe's teachings on social and economic justice from Jerome of Prague, another reformer. So he also went to study at Oxford, and became a devoted follower of Wycliffe, transplanting his ideas to eastern Europe. Hus was arrested, imprisoned and in mid-1415 he was burned at the stake. His ashes were dumped into the Rhine river.

Downstream, a century later, Martin Luther was to acknowledge the influence of Hus on the Protestant Reformation. The blood of martyrs is always the seed of the church.

G. M. Trevelyan wrote: "England was not converted from Germany but changed her own opinion, and had begun that process long before Wittenberg or Geneva became famous in theological debate."

2.3 Luther, Calvin and Tyndale

Here is not the place to delve into the various strands of the Protestant Reformation. But in Germany, France and England, these were the main figures – Martin Luther, John Calvin and William Tyndale.

It is significant that they were all very involved in Bible translation into German, French and English respectively. In recent years, we have seen a proliferation of translations after a few centuries of highest regard for the "King James version". So we tend to forget that this "authorized version" was a strategy imposed by James I to try to stop an earlier proliferation of translations. This had been happening during the Protestant Reformation. Different denominations preferred their own translation, with its peculiar nuances.

James I's mother, Elizabeth I, was the one who really consolidated the "via media" of the Anglican Church that was founded by her father Henry VIII. He had "nationalized" the church when the Pope refused to grant him a divorce to a woman who was not bearing him an heir to the throne. (Some might say that he "weaponized" the church.) He switched from Catholic to Protestant and became the Defender of the Faith in England. Unlike him, Elizabeth I was raised in that new Church of England and went to extremes to protect it - including the execution of Mary Queen of Scots, her own half-sister – who was raised a Catholic. Mary's son James, ironically, had been raised in Scotland as a hardline Presbyterian (i.e. a non-conformist). But when Elizabeth I named him as her rightful heir, he also came round to see that Anglicanism really defined what it meant to be British. So he added value to his mother's efforts to protect the Church of England by convening a huge team of translators to finalize one "authorized version".

Elizabeth not only has to fend off the threat of Catholicism, but also the "non-conformists". Groups like the Baptists, the Quakers and the Puritans were just as much of a threat, because they opposed the notion of a State Church. In fact, the English Civil War and the emergence of Oliver Cromwell almost spelled the end of the monarchy altogether. When his 40-year family dynasty ended, the Catholics made a short comeback. But public opinion basically proved to be too powerful an inertia to overcome. The king of Holland, William of Orange, was "invited" to come and invade, which he did.

When he arrived at London, though, he halted his advance and asked that Parliament validate his right to the throne. This was the beginning of the "unwritten Constitution" that exists until the present. So it is easy to see how the Protestant Reformation affected *the emergence of Democracy*. Even the translation of the Bible into the vernacular – a hallmark of evangelical churches – has had social and political impact on the cultures that were brewing nations.

In Africa, translating the Bible into different languages has played another role. Sometimes, one ethnic group became largely one-denominational, because of its Bible translation. These are called ethnically monolithic denominations. But because the intent to translate the Bible into every dialect takes a lot of time, it was overtaken by events. Suddenly at the Council of Berlin, borders were imposed on Africa. And within these borders you did not always have one culture and language. Some did, like Swaziland, Lesotho and Botswana. But South Africa is an example of a larger country, in which there were numerous ethnic groups, and thus numerous Bible translations. So this meant that multiple mission groups were at work, and thus that there are many church denominations.

In fact, the emergence of the Afrikaans Bible to a great extent distilled several creoles, which were different in Capetown, Bloemfontein and Pretoria - in spoken form - into one written language. This process took about fifty years, during which the language "hardened". It is in this respect the youngest language in the world. A visit to the Afrikaans Bible Museum in Paarl is well worth it. It is similar to what happened in Germany. Written German is one thing, but various dialects are quite another. Luther's translation of the Bible helped to consolidate a written language. And this resonated with the emergence of Germany as a nation-state, beyond the hegemony of Rome.

Luther experienced the same thing as Wycliffe, to his horror. German peasants rose up and revolted! Personal renewal always leads to social renewal, something that Luther (and many church leaders ever since) may have overlooked. South Africa's late theologian David Bosch put it this way: "Christianity that does not begin with the individual, does not begin. But Christianity that ends with the individual, ends." Forewarned is forearmed. We have to make room for the vocation of *prophets* in church leadership, to engage the powers – not just for pastors, evangelists and theologians. Here are again some highlights from Benson Bobrick in <u>Wide as the Waters</u>:

"The insurrection began in July 1524 in the Black Forest districts near the headwaters of the Danube and spread to the Rhenish provinces of Franconia, Thuringia, and Saxony. By January 1525 the entire area was in open revolt. The insurgents published a manifesto in twelve articles, studded with biblical quotation, in which they proclaimed an end to servitude, tithes, and inheritance taxes, and concluded with the words, "If we are wrong let Luther set us right."

"Among the insurgents fanatical leaders emerged. Some not only rejected the authority of the Church, but of Scripture too, and began to speak of an inward Word – a special revelation from God. "May God, in His mercy," exclaimed Luther, "preserve me from a Church in which there are only such saints,"

"The most noted of the enthusiasts was Thomas Munzer, a former Lutheran turned Anabaptist and pastor of the small town of Alstadt in Thuringia, whose exhortations were laced with apocalyptic predictions of divine intervention on the side of the oppressed.

"For a brief spell the rebels had their way. Then the nobility, recovering from their first shock, strick back with seasoned troops.

"Munzer's peasants began to sing in slowly swelling, hymnlike strains, "Come, Holy Spirit," fully expecting battling angels to descend from on high. But artillery at once opened a breach in their rude fortress and scattered death and confusion in their midst. In an instant, their resolution gave way to panic, panic to despair. They tried to flee, but there was nowhere to run to; by the end of the day five thousand had been caught and slain."

Africa has seen far more blood and gore than the Peasants' Revolts triggered by Wycliffe in England and by Luther in Germany. Naively, neither church leader seemed to expect it – they did not claim to have any political ambitions. In his book The Construction of Nationhood: Ethnicity, Religion and Nationalism, Adrian Hasting observes: "The nineteenth century protestant missionary was, above all, a Bible man... he was often to a considerable extent creating the language and, with it, a defined ethnicity." Very often, the leaders of Africa's liberation movements had church roots.

My point is rather that we cannot be blind to the social and economic conditions and aspirations of our converts and congregations. Christians are citizens too and there are political and even military or para-military organizations out there vying for their support. These allegiances are not mutually exclusive, they are overlapping. So we simply have to "engage the powers". It is the church's prophetic vocation. And this applies to all churches, not just to some.

2.4 The Radical Reformers

As I have stated, the Anabaptists were proponents of radical theological transformation. Not just change of ownership, but systemic change.

The Puritans grew into a force. Some preferred to "leave" and others to "remain". Many Puritans emigrated to the colonies of North America, indeed, government encouraged them to. But those who remained still challenged the status quo and one of them was Oliver Cromwell. For forty years, the British monarchy was "parked". But the "via media" of Anglicanism and the monarchy were remembered too fondly, and the Republican experiment ended.

That is, until the American colonies rose in defiance, and declared themselves independent. The notion of separating church and state became a founding principle in the USA. Once again the beliefs and convictions of the radical reformers were at the root of this.

In Britain, some of these radicals were called the "Levellers". Without going into detail, their military efforts contributed to the execution of Charles I. In today's parlance, especially in South Africa, we would call the "Populists".

In terms of the narrative of church history, there are Roman Catholics, moderate Reformers (basically the mainline churches) and the Radical Reformers (or non-mainline churches). This leads to another distinction that needs to be made, between three postures:

The notion of a "Christian nation" which may have rejected Rome's hegemony, but continues on with the church at the centre society, governed by a pious ruler who authorizes Bible translations and creeds as "Defender of the Faith"

The rejection of political participation, which is the Anabaptist tradition

Principled pluralism, allowing religious freedom in a non-confessional state

Speaking of the colonies of North America, there was "social space" for Mennonite groups to create enclaves within which salvation could be enjoyed by Community, but the prevailing approach of the Puritans was to respect freedom *of* religion. No one ever imagined freedom *from* religion.

South Africa is in a similar space today. It is largely a Christianized country, according to the census. So government meetings often open with a prayer, and reciting the Lord's Prayer at school is not seen as one religion dominating the others. It is seen as simply the way things are.

But there is also room for other faiths like Judaism, Islam, Hinduism and Buddhism. Toleration of these faiths is included in freedom *of* religion. But when secular religions like Humanism or Marxism try to squeeze out Christianity, that is about freedom *from* religion, and that is not part of our heritage. In China, a million Uighurs are currently being subjected to "re-education camps". When any monotheists are crushed by a secular or Marxist state, Christians should take exception.

However, to say that South Africa has always been a "non-confessional" state is probably an exaggeration. Because the reality was for centuries that the Dutch Reformed Church (DRC) was predominant. Just as the Catholic church has been in Latin America, and in Quebec. That neither precludes other churches from occupying some social space, nor does it deny the reality that society functioned that way.

Unlike Islam, Christianity did not start with any particular political model. It has flourished under persecution and floundered under predominance. Some think that the emergence of Humanism and Marxism in Europe as secular religions was because of the space they enjoyed by a church that was hopelessly divided!

South Africa still has elements of all three postures itemized above, operating in society. Perhaps this is natural in such a cosmopolitan, eclectic context?

But one thing is certain – while some denominations may recede into their enclaves, the church at large must engage the powers and preach good news to the poor.

One example of principled pluralism is the space for religious political parties to stand in elections, for seats in Parliament. For example, the Africa Christian Democratic Party. It can represent the interests of Christians (or Christianity) in governance.

This can be turned around the other way as well. On Easter morning, it is not unusual to see several political party leaders worshipping at Moria with the Zion Christian Church (ZCC). This is because that church has such a huge following across the country. While it tends to be isolated or self-contained, nevertheless politicians gravitate to that point of pilgrimage, to pay their respects. ZCC members are voters, after all!

2.5 The Anti-Slavery and Modern Missionary Movements

"Missionaries" go back as far as the Great Commission. The twelve apostles dispersed in different directions. They were not afraid to "engage the powers" as one can see from St Paul's speech to Felix at Caesarea in Acts chapter 24.

During the three centuries of persecution that followed, the church came to be known as the Third Way. This was largely because it stood for something unique – not for Roman power nor for Jewish commerce. It was reputed for taking a new stand on behalf of the poor and the vulnerable. One example was the stand that Christians took against infanticide. This had been widely practices by the Romans. Some of residents of Rome complained in Latin records about the number of dead babies floating in the Tiber river. Through awareness-raising, adoption, and in the Middle Ages the monasteries, and when they were closed after the Protestant Reformation, the invention of orphanages, the church has made the world a safer place for infants.

In the age that followed Constantine's merger of church and state, Europe gradually slipped into the so-called Dark Ages. Another famous missionary movement arose during this period, called the Peregrini. Ireland had been evangelized by St Patrick, and has been predominantly Catholic ever since. These Irish missionaries set out to re-evangelize Europe, during the Dark Ages. The Irish Church had evolved because of its isolation and the Peregrini were mainly well-to-do members of the aristocracy. So when they crossed the sea to Scotland, Holland and penetrated down as far at St Gall in Switzerland, their ministry quite naturally engaged the local authorities.

Out of the Counter-Reformation (the Catholic church's response to the Protestant Reformation) came a surge of missionary activity in the 17th century (i.e. the 1600s). Remember that the Cape Colony was first established in 1652, a full 155 years after Bartholemeu Dias first sailed around the Cape, and 152 years before the London Missionary Society was formed. In this century, Spain was the super-power of Europe. It was busy colonizing what is now called Latin America.

By 1600, the Jesuits had over 8500 missionaries operating in 23 countries. But this huge surge lost its impetus during the 18th century, because the Jesuits lost favour with Rome (which became suspicious about Jesuit ambitions). By the time of the French Revolution, the predominantly Protestant north of Europe had no such cohesive missionary force. Nor were the resources available, for a lot of Spain's expansionism was self-funded by plunder from their conquests in South America.

Sub-Saharan Africa has been evangelized mostly by the Modern Missionary Movement. It can trace its roots to the London Missionary Society, which was formed seven years after the French Revolution, in London, in 1796. This was concurrent to the Anti-Slavery Movement, and involved some of the same people. For example, as Tom Hiney recounts in his book On the Missionary Trail:

"In 1793 an India Bill went before parliament which renewed the royal license of the East India Company. The MP William Wilberforce called for an amendment allowing Christian missions and native schools to be opened in India, but the bid was resisted and not one single bishop supported the amendment when it went before the House of Lords."

Missionaries have often been critiqued for having been affiliated with colonialism. There is some truth in that because they "piggy-backed" on it, during this new era of exploration and colonialism.

But at the same time, imperial business companies were not always in favour of mission activity entering the same space overseas. One reason for this was that one missionary activity was a kind of Slavery Observatory, that fed intelligence back to the likes of William Wilberforce as he led the Anti-Slavery Movement in British parliament. This clashed outright with business interests.

Slavery is but one of many injustices that missionaries confronted as they spread out across the seven seas. Other included:

The practice of suttee in India (a widow was burned alive when her husband died, so that they could be buried together)

The practice of foot-binding in China, which left woman at a lifetime disadvantage compared to men, confining them in most cases to domestic life

Infanticide in Tahiti (remembering that this was also practiced in Rome before Christianity)

We are not going to mention the health and education services introduced by missionaries. Our focus is on advocacy and lobbying. There is no question that this prophetic vocation was part of the overall mix of ministry, right from the start of the Modern Missionary Movement.

One of the first missionaries that the London Missionary Society deployed in South Africa was Johannes van der Kemp, originally from Holland. He and a Xhosa translator named Bruntjie set out from the Cape Colony for its eastern frontier, only to find themselves in the midst of fighting between the boers and the Xhosa chieftan Gaika. The missionary went boldly to Gaika's kraal to present his credentials and state his true intentions – and he was not unwelcome. So an initial mission house was built there.

But before long, Gaika asked him to close it down because of continued fighting with the boers, so he relocated it. As the fighting spread, he had to close that second mission as well. So he took a third run at it, in the town of Graaff-Reinet, building a boarding school for the children of slaves working in and around the town.

When he began native prayer meetings in town, he started to receive death threats from the boers. One of the two new missionaries who had joined him there resigned because of this rising hostility. At one point, not less than 300 boer wagons assembled at Zwargershoek, to the extent that the nearest settlers fled from their farms. They expected an altercation between Dutch settlers and missionaries! This was only avoided by the intervention of British forces.

Not long after, boers rode into town and burned down the Khoi school. The missionary was chased away by four "hired guns" who had been paid to take him out.

From there, he moved south to Algoa Bay and started another mission, until a Dutch governor took over in Capetown. Policies changed with the return of the Dutch and van der Kemp was told to move again, to Bethelsdorp (near present-day Port Elizabeth). Tom Hiney relates more in his book <u>On the Missionary Trail</u>:

"Now that they both completely fluent in the Khoi language, Read and van der Kemp were starting to register the extent of cruelties practiced against the Hottentot people by some of the settlers. There was no free press in Capetown, nor had there ever been a court case on the frontier involving violence against a Hottentot. Much of the brutality was taking place in remote country...

"Van der Kemp and Read were now hearing a stream of accounts, in Khoi, of specific instances of killing and brutality. Read wrote urgently on the matter to the Evangelical press in England.

"In 1805 two more missionaries joined them and Governor Janssens was coming under increasing pressure to put an end to the mission. Read and van der Kemp were again summoned to Capetown, where they were detained – with their families – for several months, awaiting the governor's decision. They were not permitted to leave Capetown. The impasse was only removed in January 1806 when the British reclaimed the colony after a sea battle off Bloubeergstrand, near Capetown. Lord

Caledon was installed as governor and by March of that year van der Kemp and Read were back at Bethelsdorp.

"In 1809 Bethelsdorp was visited by a British government commissioner called Colonel Collins, who asked van der Kemp whether he would agree to send his Hottentot converts, when required, to work on neighbouring farms or for the magistrate. Van der Kemp refused and his answer was recorded in Collins's report: 'Sir, my commission is to preach, not to put chains on the legs of Hottentots and Caffers, but to preach liberty to the captives.' Back in Capetown, Collins recommended to the governor that the mission station at Bethelsdorp be closed down on the grounds that it was designed 'not to benefit the Colony, but the Hottentots'. Caledon overruled the suggestion, but pressure on the mission intensified.

"At a time when many public figures in Britain – not just Evangelical – were pushing for the freedom of existing slaves throughout the world, Read's detailed descriptions of conditions in South Africa were widely used in the debate in the British press.

"The relationship between missionaries and colonialism was never so straitforward. That they were contemporaneous forces and at times mutually useful does not mean that they were predominantly co-operative; very often they were ranged against one another, particularly over slavery. It is hard to see how men like Johannes van der Kemp, who married the widow of a Madagascan slave and had assassination attempts made on him by white settlers, could in any way be seen as a stooge of imperialism."

An historical novel was once written by Sarah Gertrude Millin about Johannes van der Kemp called <u>The Burning Man</u>.

Caledon was replaced by Sir John Craddock, who set up a circuit court in the eastern Cape. This "Black Circuit" brought a total of 58 European men and women to trial in Algoa Bay. A thousand witnesses were called – Khoi, Xhosa and European. While many cases were dismissed for lack of proof, there were some convictions. At the time, that was extraordinary.

Was this a portent of the TRC?

Sadly, not one of South Africa's eleven national languages is Khoi or San. The Ba Baroa are still being marginalized and in that sense, the work of Johannes van der Kemp is still unfinished.

2.6 How Pentecostalism came to South Africa

Negro spirituals are the lamentations of slaves. They were freed by the American Civil War, during which 750 000 soldiers lost their lives, many of them black. The base population of the USA at the time was 30 million. It was traumatic, to say the least.

Before the war, negros were only allowed to sing - they were not allowed to touch musical instruments. That is why that period is remembered for its soulful vocal music. But after the war, they had access to instruments. However, they did not always try to emulate European music, they sometimes even mocked it, and introduced some of their own African rhythms. Jazz was born.

Out of Jazz came Blues. Out of Blues came Rock n Roll. The world of music was changed forever. While this is an oversimplification, it is also a metaphor. For the same thing happened to the church. It evolved, and one of the great movements to arise after the Civil War was Pentecostalism (sometimes called the Charismatic Movement.) It had its roots in Revivalism, akin to the Methodist revival in England. Revivalism often included faith-healing. This surge can be seen as a response to the highly rational and intellectual theology of that era. The Charismatic Movement involved many blacks and women in leadership. In short, it was counter-cultural. And it has had a huge impact on church history ever since. More especially in South Africa.

Influenced by the earlier holiness movement, the National Holiness Association was formed in New Jersey in 1867. Pentecostal Christianity emphasized moral living in conjunction with special gifts from the Holy Spirit.

Many early Pentecostals were pacifists. At the outbreak of World War I, some Pentecostals called for a "great peace council" at which they could state their opposition to warfare. Every major Pentecostal denomination has at some point adopted a pacifist resolution.

By the time the American Civil War had started, there had already been some recorded charismatic experiences, but it was only after the Civil War that this phenomenon came to the fore. Of course it was controversial, seen by some as exclusivist. However, by 1906, in Middle America, the Azusa Street Revival happened. Pentecostalism then went global under William Seymour's pastorship.

The Pentecostal Holiness Church, with pre-Pentecostal roots as far back as 1879, was the first to adopt a clear Pentecostal statement of faith in 1908 (in the USA).

Among the pioneers of Pentecostalism in South Africa were an Australian faith-healer John Alexander Dowie (based in Zion, Illinois in the USA), and John G. Lake, who began work in Johannesburg in 1908. Lake founded the Apostolic Faith Mission.

The Zion Christian Church was strongly influenced by the doctrines of Dowie's Christian Catholic Church. ZCC was founded by Engenas Lekganyane in 1924. He had been educated partly by Lutherans, Anglicans and Presbyterians (all "mainline" churches). But in 1911 he joined the AFM. Then he joined a part of the AFM called the Zion Apostolic Church in 1912, and rose to be leader of its church in his home village by 1918. In 1920 he seceded and moved to Basutoland to join Edward Lion's utopian community under ZAFM (Zion Apostolic Faith Mission). He moved back home again as leader of this church in the Transvaal. He split with Lion in 1924 and found ZCC.

After he died in 1948, two distinct denominations emerged, symbolized by a bird and a star. His eldest son Edward continues to be the head of the original ZCC. His younger son Joseph has launched St. Engenas Zion Christian Church in 1949. Both are located on the same mountain at Moria, in Limpopo province. ZCC has now moved to a third generation of family leadership. Barnabas, a son of Edward has taken over ZCC, and Engenas (named after his grand-father) has taken over at St Engenas ZCC.

2.7 African-initiated churches

ZCC is now by far the biggest Christian denomination in South Africa, and has spread into neighbouring countries of southern Africa as well.

One can speak of both the Christianization of Africa and also the Africanization of Christianity.

Similarly, one can speak of the evangelicalization of Pentecostalism and the pentecostalization of evangelicalism.

While speaking of terminology, it is important to make another distinction. Here is what Paul Freston writes in Evangelicals and Politics in Asia, Africa and Latin America:

"Evangelicalism and fundamentalism have a complex relationship. While there is overlap (some evangelicals are fundamentalists), evangelicalism is an older and broader tendency within Protestantism, while the 'fundamentalist' label has been extended in another direction to include phenomena from other religions. Fundamentalism and evangelicalism relate differently to globalization, the former being more properly a reactive phenomenon of globalization whereas the latter predates and possibly contributes to it."

Freston points out that in the South, there are evangelicals who are currently inclined to the Left wing of politics as well to the Right wing. So the term "fundamentalist" especially as it is usually understood in terms of the American Right is definitely not synonymous with "evangelical".

Like ZCC, these churches tend to be multi-ethnic, welcoming blacks from different tribes and nations, but not so much multi-racial. This is a departure from the early roots of Pentecostalism. So is the fact that men predominate in leadership. Put another way, it is predominantly African.

Because these churches are very autonomous and self-contained, they do not tend to engage in public affairs. ZCC members are reputed to be honest and reliable employees. They still take holiness seriously.

However, these churches also promote the prophetic vocation. No so much in terms of engaging societal structures, as in engaging the "principalities and powers (the rulers of the darkness of this world)". For we wrestle not against flesh and blood – as St Paul teaches in Ephesians chapter 6. Paul Freston explains:

"It is unrealistic to expect churches of the poor, without foreign connections, to play the same role in opposition to authoritarian regimes as mainline churches."

On this note, Bishop Edward Lekganyane made something of a tactical blunder in 1985 when he invited then-President Botha to attend Easter worship at Moria. On that occasion, Botha spoke from Romans chapter 13 where St Paul teaches Christians to respect the authorities. This did not sit well with the ANC which was still banned and in exile at the time. The bishop had a lot of fence-mending to do.

But because the denomination to a great extent keeps to itself and its own ways, there was an almost fatalistic "fit" to the apartheid system. Just as missionaries had something of an ambiguous relationship with colonialism, ZCC had a fatalistic relationship with apartheid! Its founder Engenas died in 1948, the same year that the Nats were elected and that we started to see Grand Apartheid unpacked. During that forty-year period, ZCC grew incrementally into a significant force. In fact, today one would expect to see several top leaders at Moria for Easter morning worship, when over one million of its members make a pilgrimage to either the bird or the star side of the mountain.

Members can go to Moria for "interventions". These are usually with a prophet. My personal experience is that they have incredibly accurate insights. They give good advice, but it is more than "active listening" or Counseling. They operate under the prophetic vocation, which is not only one of the offices of church leadership, but one of the charismatic gifts as well. But they should not be confused with clairvoyants or fortune-tellers, who claim to have foresight. Prophets have *insight*.

We would welcome more of a public voice for these denominations, who are practicing the prophetic vocation on a day-to-day basis.

2.8 The Prosperity Doctrine

Sadly, for many of these denominations, the focus has become Prosperity not Justice. Preaching good news to the poor should not be confused with dreaming dreams of wealth and affluence. (Remember Simon Magus in Acts chapter 8.) Just like gambling and lotteries rob the poor, according to research, draining away what little wealth they have... holding up Prosperity as a goal is disingenuous. It only muddies the waters of baptism.

For example, opportunity knocks in Land Reform for the poor to rise out of poverty. But the politics around Land Reform are a kind of mine-field. The church's voice should be speaking its message of "Jubilee principles" into this great debate, rather than luring poor people to church by dreams of striking it rich. "Get-rich quick schemes" are not the answer. The poor need access to means of production, so that they can work hard. God helps those who help themselves.

1. The Prophetic Vocation

Kierkegaard once wrote: "God creates out of nothing. Wonderful, you say! But He does what is still even more wonderful – he creates saints out of sinners". Evangelists preach and convert.... Teachers educate and train.... Pastors do weddings and funerals... We should not overlook the important role of Prophets in this miracle of making saints out of sinners.

As stated above, prophecy is not to be confused with foretelling the future. It is about discernment and guidance. It may at times involve exorcism - casting out demons. It is both one of the offices of church leadership, listed repeatedly in the Bible, and also one of the charismatic gifts. On these two counts, the prophetic vocation should be taken more seriously than it tends to be.

St Paul writes repeatedly about the prophetic vocation. There is not much that one can add:

"So Christ himself gave the apostles, the prophets, the evangelists, the pastors and teachers, to equip his people for works of service, so that the body of Christ may be built up..." Ephesians 4: 11 - 12

"We have different gifts, according to the grace given to each of us. If your gift is prophesying, then prophesy in accordance with your faith..." Romans 12: 6

"To one there is given through the Spirit a message of wisdom, to another a message of knowledge by means of the same Spirit, to another faith by the same Spirit, to another gifts of healing by that one Spirit, to another miraculous powers, to another prophecy, to another distinguishing between spirits, to another speaking in different kinds of tongues, and to still another the interpretation of tongues." I Corinthians 12: 8 – 10

3.1 Old Testament Major and Minor prophets

Would Jeremiah or Amos have kept quiet about a raging issue like Land Reform?

The Methodist Church of South Africa organized an *Unburdening Panel* to hear from its members about State Capture (i.e. corruption and patronage). Its report has proved very useful in the mix of inputs that are gradually healing this maladie in our government. Here is an example of a similar confrontation in the theocracy of Israel:

"So the Lord sent Nathan to David. Nathan came to him and said, "There were two men in a certain city. One was rich, and the other was poor. The rich man had a very large number of sheep and cows, but the poor man had only one little female lamb that he had bought. He raised her, and she grew up in his home with his children. She would eat his food and drink from his cup. She rested in his arms and was like a daughter.

"Now, a visitor came to the rich man. The rich man thought it would be a pity to take one of his own sheep or cattle to prepare a meal for the traveler. So he took the poor man's lamb and prepared her for the traveler."

David burned with anger against the man. "I solemnly swear, as the Lord lives," he said to Nathan, "the man who did this certainly deserves to die! And he must pay back four times the price of the lamb because he did this and had no pity."

"You are the man!" Nathan told David.

It takes both creativity and courage to speak truth to power.

3.2 The New Covenant

In Acts chapter 15, the Council of Jerusalem unfolds. Christianity is emerging as a new world religion, out of Judaism. The bishop at this point in time appears to be James, the brother of Jesus. Peter also speaks, but his contribution is historical, about the Identity of the church.

Paul and Barnabas are focused on church Strategy – on the "way forward". But what they have to say is more insight than foresight. They recount what they have observed going on in the here-and-now in Antioch, and they interpret those events, and their relevance. This is what it is to speak prophetically.

This happens in the context of an "indaba" – not in an oracle or trance of some kind. But prophecy is more than just analysis, it is "discernment and resistance in a world of domination". That phrase is the slogan of Walter Wink's book Engaging the Powers. He writes:

"Discernment does not entail esoteric knowledge, but rather the gift of seeing reality as it really is. Nothing is more rare, or more truly revolutionary, than an accurate description of reality...

"The Roman empire had brought peace to a fratricidal world. It presided over a period of unparalleled prosperity (for the prosperous). Its might was so legendary that a single emissary could prompt surrender. But this façade of magnificence was bought at a horrible price. The revelation that comes to John strips off the mask of benevolence and reveals, beneath it, the true spirit of Rome...

"How then can the church carry on the struggle with the Powers more effectively? How can it shake off the suffocating weight of institutional self-preservation and make a difference in the world? How can it engage the Powers with the redemptive power of the cross? What kinds of action and spirituality must it cultivate to be able to serve God in the redemption of the Powers?

3.3 The Church Fathers

Here are some examples of thorny issues that the early church had to confront:

Tertullian

In Carthage, in the Roman province of Africa, he was trained as both a lawyer and a priest. He broke the force of false charges such as that Christians sacrificed infants at the celebration of the Lord's Supper and committed incest. He pointed to the commission of such crimes in the pagan world and then proved by the testimony of Pliny that Christians pledged themselves not to commit murder, adultery, or other crimes. He was the first recorded writer to refer to the Trinity.

He challenged the inhumanity of pagan customs such as feeding the flesh of gladiators to beasts. He argued that because there are no "gods" thus there is no pagan religion against which Christians may offend. Christians do not engage in the foolish worship of the emperors, they do better - they pray for them. Christians can afford to be put to torture and to death, and the more they are cast down the more they grow...

"The blood of the martyrs is seed" (Apologeticum, 50)

Perpetua and Felicitas

Rarely have women been venerated by so many, for so long! A 22-year noble woman and a pregnant slave girl were martyred together under the persecution of Septimus. In Carthage a magnificent basilica was afterwards erected over the tomb of these two women martyrs, the Basilica Maiorum, where an ancient inscription bearing their names has been found.

Saints Felicitas and Perpetua are two of seven women commemorated by name in the second part of the Canon of the Mass.

The once-flowering rambling rose "Félicité et Perpétue" (R. sempervirens x 'Old Blush') with palest pinks buds opening nearly white, was introduced by Robert Jacques in 1828.

Two historical fiction novels have been written from the point of view of Perpetua. Amy Peterson's Perpetua: A Bride, A Martyr, A Passion (ISBN 978-0972927642[1]) was published in 2004, and Malcolm Lyon's The Bronze Ladder (ISBN 978-1905237517[2]) in 2006.

"See that pot lying there?" she asked her father. "Can you call it by any other name than what it is?" "Of course not," he answered. Perpetua responded, "Neither can I call myself by any other name than what I am—a Christian."

Cyprian

A new persecution of the Christians began in under Emperor Valerian I, and both Pope Stephen I and his successor, Sixtus II suffered martyrdom at Rome.

In Africa Cyprian courageously prepared his people for the expected edict of persecution by pastoral letter, and himself set an example when he was brought before the Roman proconsul of Carthage, Aspasius Paternus. He refused to sacrifice to the pagan deities.

The consul banished him to Curubis, modern Korba. From there he comforted to the best of his ability his flock and his banished clergy. In a vision he saw his approaching fate. When a year had passed he was recalled and kept under house arrest, in expectation of severer measures after a new and more stringent imperial edict arrived, demanding the execution of all Christian clerics.

He was imprisoned at the behest of the new proconsul Galerius Maximus. The day following he was examined for the last time and sentenced to die by the sword. His only answer was *"Thanks be to God!"*

1.   http://en.wikipedia.org/wiki/Special:BookSources/9780972927642
2.   http://en.wikipedia.org/wiki/Special:BookSources/9781905237517

"He can no longer have God for his Father who has not the Church for his mother" (De unitate ecclesiae)

St Athanasius

At the age of 27, he assisted Bishop Alexander at the Council of Nicaea, where his influence began to be felt. Five months later, on his death bed, the bishop recommended Athanasius as his successor. He was elected unanimously 5 months later, and at age 30 he became archbishop of Alexandria. He was the chief defender of Trinitarianism against Arianism.

His refusal to tolerate the Arian heresy led to many trials and persecutions. He spent seventeen of the forty-six years of his episcopate in exile. During his lifetime he was engaged in theological and political struggles against the Emperors Constantine the Great and Constantius II and powerful and influential Arian churchmen, led by Eusebius of Nicomedia. Thus he came to be known as *"Athanasius Contra Mundum"*.

"Jesus that I know as my Redeemer cannot be less than God"

St. Augustine

He came from cosmopolitan Hippo, in North Africa. As a foodbasket for the capital city of the Empire, it had a thriving Roman presence. There was also a long established Hebrew community there, from which some Biblical figures had emerged – like Barnabas, his sister Mary and her son Mark. Then there was "the Third Way" – the Christian community - which Augustine refused to join for decades, in spite of his mother's prodding and prayers.

Augustine's influence is almost without comparison in church history. At its root is a personal conversion. An about face. A change of heart and mind. The basis of social renewal is personal renewal. As a changed person, Augustine set about to change the church and society.

"God loves each of us as if there were only one of us."

3.4 Ecumenical Councils

The Council of Jerusalem has already been mentioned. After the un-banning of the church by the Emperor Constantine, church councils were held more frequently and more openly. In fact, they became quite tumultuous at times – because of the controversies that they were trying to iron out.

A review of the first seven church councils indicates that the church was focusing more on itself and less on society. There were huge debates over church structure, theological nuances, heresies, the canon of scriptures to be adopted, and details of worship. Something had been misplaced in the transformation from an underground church to a state church. I am not saying that these matters are unimportant. But the focus on social and economic issues had been lost. Perhaps because the church had married the state, and the bride did not want to criticize her husband?

3.5 World Council of Churches – 1987 Conference

The WCC holds conferences every five years, rotating the setting to different cities. Its 1987 Conference was held in Ottawa, Canada.

The Dutch Reformed Church of South Africa had by this time been confronted about its general support for apartheid. Of course there had always been dissenting voices within the DRC, and even splits over this issue.

Nevertheless, the church on this occasion confessed that apartheid was heretical, and pledged to abandon its teaching of it.

So although this manifested itself as an internal "housekeeping" issue within the church body, it also represented a sea-change for every-day life in South Africa. This deep confession had to come first, followed by the un-banning of the ANC, the release of political prisoners, free and fair elections, and agreement on a Constitution.

1. Church Offices

The purpose of this section is to position the Prophetic Vocation within its natural habitat – church leadership.

4.1 Pastors

From their pulpits, they preach the relevance of religion within society. If they preach from the Bible (i.e. expository preaching), they look first at the *meaning* of a text, then at its *significance*.

Pastoring also involves Counseling. Pastoral visits, home visits, "active listening" and so forth are part of pasturing a flock.

4.2 Evangelists

On the streets and along the highways and byways they preach Renewal. This starts with personal renewal, but does not stop there – it continues into social renewal. For "no man is an island". We are social beings. *Umuntu ngamuntu ngabantu.* ("A person is a person because of other people".) South Africa's social architecture also needs renewal.

4.3 Teachers

Sometimes they are called "theologians". Daniel Berrigan made an important point that "radical action requires radical contemplation.

"Street theology" is closer to the people. Theologians sometimes abide in ivory towers.

4.4 Bishops

Already in Acts chapter 15, cited above, there appears to be a "primus inter pares" (first among equals). In that case it was James. Significantly, he spoke last, and looked for consensus among the previous speakers in what he concluded. This is very much in tune with African tradition. Decision-making in African democracy tends to try to eliminate dissent, rather than voting to find a majority.

4.5 Archbishops and Popes

Desmond Tutu was the first black archbishop of South Africa, and I believe that Pope Francis (an Argentinian) may be the first Pope from the South.

4.6 Deacons

St Stephen was one of those Seven chosen in the New Testament to assist the poor, so that the Twelve could focus on preaching and teaching. Certainly a division of roles and responsibilities emerged in the early church. More so than other church offices, this one has been more gender inclusive. For it has never been uncommon to meet deaconesses as well as deacons.

Please note that I include compassionate ministry, relief and development programming as part of the "Diaconate". However, I do not include the ministry of Justice or Peacemaking.

4.7 Prophets

This list is recited to help position the Prophetic Vocation in its proper place. To my way of thinking, a prophet becomes (quoting Daniel Berrigan again) "a witness against the culture".

The church needs specialists who have this spiritual gifting as well, to articulate its challenges in the corridors of power ("to speak truth to power"). It also needs to designate Prophets among its leaders.

Perhaps we tend to call them "activists" or even "protesters"?

4.8 Prayer

I am mentioning this on purpose. Some people withdraw or retire and devote themselves to prayer.

However, prayer is really cross-cutting. It is incumbent on all Christians to pray. The Lord's Prayer is short and simple – only 52 words (in English). That is the prayer that Jesus taught when asked to teach us how to pray. This is because his followers noted that he had a visible "prayer life".

4.9 The Laity

This is the traditional word for the "people sitting in the pews". A K A believers, followers, adherents, members, etc

There is a Franciscan prayer for the flock:

"May God bless you with discomfort
At easy answers, half-truths, and superficial relationships
So that you may live deep within your heart
"May God bless you with anger
At injustice, oppression, and exploitation of people
So that you may work for justice, freedom and peace
"May God bless you with tears
To shed for those who suffer pain, rejection, hunger and war
So that you may reach out your hand to comfort them
And turn their pain into joy
"And may God bless you with enough foolishness
To believe that you can make a difference in the world
So that you can do what others claim cannot be done
To bring justice and kindness to all our children and the poor."

1. Eras

This short section is merely to establish a framework for what comes later...

5.1 The Persecuted Church

Starting with Jesus himself, the "People of the Way" were persecuted by both the Jews and the Romans. This went on for about three centuries. During such periods, of course, it is very hard for the church to try to influence public policy.

Persecution has not stopped altogether. In fact, in parts of Africa, the Christian church is still "under the gun" so to speak. As it was in Angola, Mozambique and Ethiopia during the Cold War, when these three countries were under communist rule. Those who survived can tell many tales about persecution. Today this treatment is still true in Muslim countries.

So while the church in these countries cannot speak truth to power, it is important for the world-wide church to speak out against persecution. Freedom of worship should be enjoyed everywhere.

5.2 Theocracy

Even Rome after Constantine did not return to the pure Old Testament model. It rather combined church and state in an alliance. However the term "Calvinist theocracy" was used in the period when John Calvin ruled Geneva, during the Protestant Reformation.

"Reconstructionists" are a sub-set of Calvanists who believe that the church has a remit to rebuild society along theocratic lines.

5.3 Separation of church and state

In his book Evangelical and Politics in Asia, Africa and Latin America, Paul Freston notes:

"With regard to church-state relations, few Third World contexts have anything similar to the United States tradition of separation. In the US, this tradition is so strong that it constrains all religious actors in politics, whether their doctrine tends in this direction or not (as Tocqueville commented on American Catholicism in the 1830s). Where this tradition is absent, the room for disagreement between religious actors in politics is much greater; and where the existing nation-state itself is questioned, the gap is still wider."

5.4 Religious Pluralism

Since 1994, South Africa has definitely entered a new era of tolerance, marred from time to time by outbreaks of xenophobia.

At the World Council of Churches, the focus on Racism turned from the Holocaust in 1948, when the State of Israel was established, to Apartheid. That same year was when the Nats entered government. Their defeat in the Anglo-Boer War was a distant memory; they lost that war, but they won the peace. Soon the pillars of grand apartheid were put in place, and the church had an on-going role to play in the struggle against Racism. The WCC's focus on Racism changed from germany to South Africa.

It was because of this background, that Durban was chosen to be the venue for the International Conference on Racism, Xenophobia and Intolerance, in 2001. It seemed like the optimal place to agree in international standards to keep Racism in check. However, the earlier success in the "rainbow nation" was severely tempered by the Rwandan genocide, which happened in April 1994. Ironically, the very same month that the first free and fair elections were held in South Africa. This genocide tarnished the reputation of blacks, illuminating that they could be perpetrators as well as victims. (The Hutus and the Tutsis are not just different tribes, they are different races as well – Bantu and Nilotic respectively.)

5.5 Democracy

This "political science" tends to be defined as free-and-fair elections, leading to an open parliament that rules supreme.

South Africa has arrived. It has one of the best Constitutions in the world. It has national, provincial, district and local levels of government. It has a multi-party system.

Curiously, both traditional rights and human rights are entrenched in its Constitution. These sometimes clash. For example, the legal prohibition of prostitution as it stands does not line up with the Bill of Rights in the Constitution. This gives rise to great debate between two positions: "partial decriminalization" and "full decriminalization". The so-called Nordic strategy of partial decriminalization (i.e. going after the men who pay) probably aligns best with Christian views. It is also the predominant view amongst Feminists world-wide. But there is controversy.

5.6 Humanism and Marxism

These two secular religions are eroding away at Christian beliefs and convictions in South Africa, as they have already done elsewhere. Just as traditional rights at times clash with human rights, so also at times Christian views clash with Humanist or Marxist views. This is why it is so important that the church not lose its voice.

In the great debate about Land Reform, Marxists are very vocal that they would like to see all land owned by the State. Could it be for this reason that for ten years or so, ANC government policy has resisted transferring title of land to even black farmers? This was codified in the State Land Lease and Disposal Policy of 2013. The aim has been to pass on "access" to assets, not property in any real sense.

However, this was recently challenged in the courts by *a black farmer*, who won! The court instructed government to transfer the title of the land that he had been leasing – for almost 30 years! – into his name.

Land rights are complicated. However, the numbers are overwhelming. The official count is that 6.7 million citizens are out of work – who could be in the work force. The real number is probably close to ten million. This is a 29 percent unemployment rate. By comparison, during the Great Depression in North America, unemployment peaked at 13 percent - in 1933. That was the worst year of the "dirty thirties".

My contention is that the church could mitigate the steps that government is taking to expropriate land without compensation, by the formation of a JUBILEE LAND BANK. Call it a charm offensive.

5.7 A Secular State

Most people probably view South Africa today as a secular state. This is not reality.

God created the world, and he still owns it – including South Africa. There are both supernatural and natural Powers – seen and unseen – that would like everyone to think otherwise. The Domination System will even try to convince citizens that there is no God.

I do not believe that God ever needs our help. Rather, we always need His help. Great leaders like John Dube and Albert Luthuli lived through tough times as they rose to prominence. Walter Sisulu and Nelson Mandela were layers, and thus privileged among the populace. But they did not choose a life on Easy Street. They were ready to die for their beliefs and convictions. We need to rise to the challenges of our time, and preach good news to the poor.

1. Who are these Powers?

This is not the place to delve deep into any of them, but just to note them and distinguish between them. Part of the key to unlock solutions, is to discern what the nature of the problems really is. Take any problem and ask – is it flesh and blood? Principalities and powers? Structural causes?

6.1 "Principalities and Powers... the rulers of the darkness of this world"

St Paul mentions these in Ephesians chapter 6. Engaging them is often called "spiritual warfare". It can get heavier than that, even into Exorcism.

In the great debate about Land Reform, I have no doubt that the Adversary would like to sow confusion and acrimony into it. One of the main roles that the church can play is to cool of the debate rhetoric. Let cooler heads prevail. The issues are complex, and there are different sides to the story. We are all South African citizens or residents, so we need to find one another on this.

6.2 "Flesh and blood"

In emphasizing that there is also a struggle going on in the "heavenlies", St Paul is re-visiting an ethical dualism that goes all the way back to Zoroaster, even before Old Testament times. But it also creeps into the Old Testament, for example, in the Prologue to the Book of Job. Job's life and experience in "flesh and blood" plays out against a dialogue in the court of heaven between the Lord and his Adversary. These are an early version of multiple plot lines.

The phrase from the Lord's Prayer comes to mind: "Lead me not into temptation, but deliver me from evil". Let us face honestly the fact that in the great debate about Land Reform, there are huge vested interests. A lot is at stake.

Concerns about Food Security are not entirely unfounded, either, when you think about the way that Zimbabwe went. And hunger is a "flesh and blood" issue.

6.3 Structural causes

There are also policies and party platforms that come into play. Deeper than that are cultural practices and traditions.

When we face any problem, we have to assess whether to deal with the superficial symptoms, or the deeper causes. This can take a lot of wisdom. Dealing with the symptoms can be just a quick fix. Dealing with the causes and structures can bring more enduring changes.

On the question of Land Reform, we need to bear in mind the history of southern Africa in this respect. Willem Saaymen summarizes it well in his book the <u>History of Christian Mission in South Africa</u>:

"I guess it is by now a well-known fact that the Western concept of individual ownership of land was mostly foreign to Africans. Africa tribes 'owned' land communally and, according to their pastoral and nomadic lifestyle, regarded land as 'theirs' also while they might not have been occupying it at a given time. There is a Herero saying which expresses this view well: Wherever our cattle's feet have trodden, there is Herero land. Western capitalist colonialists with their concept of individual ownership of land, of individuals being able to buy and sell tracts of land, which then excluded the original African 'owners' of the land, were therefore unavoidably set on a collision course with Africans about this issue." (p 28)

"Again the dispossession of land did not come about by accident. There was a good economic reason, according to the capitalist system being introduced, why Africans had to leave their land. The exploitation of the Colony depended on the availability of cheap Black labour. As long as the Africans had land (and cattle), they could exist independently by way of successful subsistence farming. As soon as they were dispossessed of land, they became dependent on the colonists (and missionaries) for their livelihood. Black South Africans were therefore increasingly forced off their land to supply the cheap labour needed by the growing capitalist system (cf. Bruwer 1988:59-62)" (p 30).

Land Reform is a complex issue. There are constitutional issues, technical issues in terms of agriculture, related business issues and pervading ideologies as well.

The church cannot solve the conundrum, but it can contribute to finding a fair and just balance.

6.4 Prophetic "interventions"

I have found that both ZCC and St Engenas ZCC take this kind of discernment very seriously, when you rock up at Moria for an "intervention".

Prophets have consultation rooms there. But there are no desks, or even chairs. There are just mats on the floor. You sit and talk. The prophet stays prostrate – listening and praying. Then he will address you. He gives advice. He has heard many cases before, remember, just like a doctor. It may be the first time for you that a certain ailment afflicts you, but the doctor has no doubt encountered it previously. Probably more than once. This is true of practicing prophets too.

I am not saying that we should imitate this exact methodology. What impresses me is that a place has been prepared, with registration, a waiting room, and numerous consultation rooms. In short, they take the prophetic vocation very seriously.

My worry is whether the churches are yet prepared to "speak truth to power" about Land Reform?

6.5 Counseling

There is certainly space in ministry for psychology as well. It is a profession in its own right, like nursing or medicine, teaching or giving legal advice. All of these are important.

Courses are also available for lay people in "Christian listening". This plays a very helpful role in assisting people to find their own solutions to their problems.

But these are different from the ministry of Justice.

Education and Health are also important church ministries. In Zimbabwe, most rural health care is still delivered to the people by mission hospitals. The government health institutions are mainly in urban areas. In Malawi, most Primary Schooling is still delivered by church organizations. In South Africa, Christian schools and hospitals are not entirely unknown, although less common than they once were.

But the church must never lose its prophetic voice:

"When they take you before synagogues and magistrates and authorities, do not worry about how to defend yourselves or what to say, because when the time comes, the Holy Spirit will teach you what you must say." (Luke 12: 11-12)

1. Tendencies of Democracy

In his book Evangelicals and Politics in Asia, Africa and Latin America, Paul Freston asks a probing question:

"Can the churches move from conflict with autocratic governments into being schools for 'high intensity democracy'?"

He also makes some interesting distinctions and comments. These are relevant to our missive:

- There is "transitioning to democracy" and also "consolidating democracy"

60

- Electoral democracy is different from liberal democracy
- "democracy based on a hive of voluntary associations"
- "the likely effects on democracy of any specific manifestation of voluntaristic Christianity"
- "globalization from below"

Freston has a lot to say about Voluntarism in general, Alexis de Tocqueville in particular, and he recognizes that it is part of the evangelical mix in the Third World. However, it is not the predominant tendency, as it was and is in the USA. Because the separation of church and state is nowhere as deeply entrenched as in America.

The Christianization of South Africa took place over centuries. While the Dutch Reformed Church was predominant in this endeavour, that was not to the exclusion of other missions. In other words, the notion of "Calvinist theocracy" was blended with other tendencies. One strong influence was "voluntaristic Christianity", akin to what Alexis de Tocqueville journalistically reported on in the pioneering days of the USA. And in the era since 1994, in South Africa, probably the more prevalent tendency has been "principled pluralism" - allowing religious freedom in a non-confessional state.

I keep repeating that there is a difference between freedom OF religion and freedom FROM religion. South African citizens are by and large very devout people of faith. So our challenge in this new dispensation is not to let Humanism and/or Marxism supplant Christian values.

I was intrigued by another comment by Freston:

"Such variety is perhaps not surprising in view of the classical sociologists' analyses of evangelical religion. Engels thought Protestantism was often at the service of the bourgeoisie, but could at times be revolutionary, albeit (for him) in an unrealistic way. Weber saw it as unintentionally promoting a capitalist rationality in tension with the

ethic of universal love. Tocqueville viewed popular Protestantism as having a basic role in democratization."

7.1 Despotic Democracy

This term has been used a lot of late – including about South Africa – but not only. It was actually used by Alexis de Tocqueville! But it has been resurrected in recent years.

According to research units like Civicus, there is a world-wide tightening up on "civil society". The era of the "vindictive triumphalists" under ex-President Zuma was really down on NGOs. Minister of State Security David Mahlobo repeatedly used the term "dangerous NGOs", even in Parliament. Any church with foreign connections can be seen through paranoid lenses as letting in Trojan horses. This is nothing more than a variation of conspiracy theories.

But what the Puritans and other wanted when they left the Old World for the New World, was an end to despotic rule of any kind. This is precisely why civil society became so strong and vibrant.

In 1994, many cadres of South Africa's civil society departed into government – where they had not been welcome before. There has been a new generation of civil society leaders rising up. Among these are many devout Christians. But ironically, they no longer work for church agencies, or even in Christian organizations. I will not name names, but in the ranks of Save South Africa, a loose formation of NGOs, you find many women and men of faith. Up to an including CEOs.

Africa's archetypical strongman leader figured out how to run a democracy and stay in power. Despotic democracy became a window-dressing for top-down leadership.

Thus Freston explains the difference between electoral democracy and liberal democracy:

"The former is a minimal framework (regular, fair and free elections), while the latter includes a deeper institutional structure of freedoms, civilian control over the military, accountability of office-holder and the

rule of law through an independent judiciary. While 61 per cent of governments met the former definition in 1996, only 41 per cent met the latter; in fact, the latter was losing ground outside the developed world."

State Capture happened because "vindictive triumphalists" could not be held in check. This term was introduced by Mashele and Qobo as far back as 2013.

It may be a thumbsuck, but I would call the period of 1994 - 2008 "transitioning to democracy" and the decade of 2009 – 2019 "consolidating democracy".

Church participation in the journey to Justice has been mixed - probably because of the eclectic mix of church denominations, each with its own tendency. But that recalls another insight from Paul Freston:

"For many who had lost faith in the state following the collapse of the Eastern bloc, and who did not believe that the market left to its own devices could produce democracy, the revitalization of civil society seemed the way forward. This was the rediscovery of an ancient tradition, dating back at least to Tocqueville. For some in that tradition, voluntary associations, below the level of the state but above the individual and the family, promote pluralism and democracy regardless of whether they are concerned explicitly with public affairs."

It is not my intention to promote one tendency or another. I am not prescribing, I am describing. South Africa has a mix, in which some churches are more inclined and others are less inclined to send emissaries into the corridors of power.

What I am saying is that our work is never over, it just changes. So the prophetic vocation continues to be mission-critical in making sure that good news is preached to the poor.

1. Comparative Levels of Public Engagement

The Society for the Abolition of the Slave Trade was an NGO established in 1787, in London. The influence of the Quakers was a driving force.

Slavery was abolished by British parliament in 1807, twenty years later. Obviously during this period and thereafter, there was a high level of engagement by churches in the Anti-Slavery Movement.

But slave-owners were also Christians.

One famous missionary was David Livingstone. He believed that Slavery would only really come to an end with higher levels of economic development "at source". This is similar to the slogan that we often hear today: "Trade, not Aid". So Livingstone was an explorer, seeking our trade routes, business prospects and investment opportunities.

He was also another Slavery Observatory, often coming into direct contact in Africa's interior with slavers. This was in the 19th century, long after Johannes van der Kemp in the 18th century, and deeper north into what is now Botswana, and beyond.

Livingstone was also with the London Missionary Society, but he was a Congregationalist. Out of this church in the general area of the famous mission Tiger Kloof emerged the late great Albert Luthuli in the 20th century. Another churchman with a prophetic vocation.

One can mention Slavery in the same breath as dispossession of land, urbanization and even genocide. In those days, in South Africa, whites could get a hunting license to kill blacks.

For a moment I jump back to the present day. I went looking for a new book when I saw it advertised on-line. It is called <u>Al Capones of Mpumalanga – The Bad and Good Political Figures,</u> written by David Dube. I dropped into the Christian book store at a mall near my home. I asked if they had it. The reply that I got was a wake-up call: "We only sell Christian books".

How can we sell the Solution, if we haven't analysed and understood the Problem? My paraphrase of the answer I got is: "We only sell the Solution. We don't 'do' Problems." I was non-plussed, but it said a lot about the very narrow view of Christian outreach that some believers have.

8.1 Pre-Union period (1807 – 1913)

The framework I have adopted is very arbitrary. It begins with the Abolition of Slavery by British parliament. But in took almost another century to stamp it out world-wide. Other than David Livingstone's exploration of central Africa, what was going on in South Africa during this period?

The term "missionary" came to have a very different connotation in main-stream South Africa, than it did for non-mainline missionary societies like the LMS...

In this country the boers were and still are very religious. Every town built a church with a steeple. All the farmers attended these Dutch Reformed churches and from time to time, their farms were visited by their pastor. That is, the man who preached to them on Sundays from the pulpit in the church, in their Afrikaans language.

But each and every church also had a "missionary". Another man, whose role was to evangelize "the blacks" and minister to them. So when the pastor halted his horse and buggy in front of the boer's house on a pastoral visit, he was always accompanied by another white man, who would not go into the farmer's house. He would meet with all the black workers. "Out behind the barn."

You can give some credit to other mission efforts just as they operated in all African countries, but this country is different. White people went to church and every church supported a "missionary" as well as a pastor. To a very great extent, these missionaries are the ones who have made South Africa what it still is spiritually – a place where God is worshipped widely. *By all races.*

Having said that, you can also see the roots of apartheid in this approach of "Calvinist theocracy".

8.2 Pre-Apartheid (1913 – 1948)

I have chosen the date of the Natives' Land Act to start this period, following the Anglo-Boer War. Up to the year that the Nats were elected.

By 1913, the translation of the Bible into Afrikaans was closing in on completion. This was having the effect of hardening several different creoles that combined Dutch with other languages including French and Portuguese.

In 1915, the Dutch Reformed Church started pressing for the prohibition of mixed marriages. These had never been out-lawed, in fact some pioneer missionaries like Johannes van der Kemp had married African (non-white) women. This practice had always been discouraged, but it had never been formally out-lawed. Now, gradually, even the prevailing practice among the mission societies was to discourage inter-racial marriage.

The prophetic themes of this period were:

- Land policy
- Mission domination
- The peddling of white culture, not just Christianity

Remember that Nelson Mandela was born in this period, in 1918. Many of these prophetic themes are reminiscent of his autobiography Long Walk To Freedom. So by 1948, Madiba was 30 years old. That year he was elected national secretary of the ANC Youth League, which he had co-founded four years earlier. He would be elected ANCYL president three years later in 1951.

Let's be honest, there is a different between church action and the individual action of Christians.

Some churchmen like Trevor Huddleston were exemplary in their prophetic vocation. But not all. Huddleston arrived in Johannesburg from England in 1943. In 1954 he gave Hugh Masekela his first trumpet. In 1959 he co-founded the Anti-Apartheid Movement (AAM) with Julius Nyerere. He became a bishop in Tanzania in 1960. In 1988 he and Archbishop Desmond Tutu addressed a rally of 200 000 people in Hyde Park, London. These are just some highlights of someone who takes their prophetic vocation seriously.

Father Huddleston died on 20 April 1998 at his home in England. His ashes were interred next to the Church of Christ the King in Sophiatown.

8.3 Grand Apartheid (1948 – 1982)

More than any other period, because of the weight of oppression experienced, this period illuminates the differences in church exhortation. The main challenges were:

- Bantustans
- Pass-laws
- Banning of mixed marriages
- Banning of mixed worship
- Weaponizing the church
- Forced removals and segregation of once eclectic communities
- Bantu education
- One man one vote

Prominent responses of churches and Christians included:

- Marches (e.g. the Women's march in 1956 and the infamous march in Sharpville in 1960)
- Burning pass-books
- Conscientious objection to military service

But the regime fought back, for example by banning the Christian Institute of Beyers Naude.

Here are some highlights, focusing specifically on the wide range of church responses:

Anglican & Methodist churches mixed opposition with compliance

Since 1948, ZCC youth were free to participate in 'African political movements' as long as these did not conflict with ZCC practices

1974 Belydende Kring (BK was a dissident group within the DRC) claimed that blacks were "held hostage theologically and politically"

1977 Beyers Naude and his Christian Institute were banned

Scripture Union started multi-racial camps

1978 Election of a black archbishop of a mainline church (i.e. Desmond Tutu)

Uniting Church (blacks and coloreds) rejected the homelands policy

AFM cut off funding to Frank Chikane's church for being involved in politics

1981 Presbyterian Church of SA voted to defy the Group Areas Act and the Mixed Marriages Act

UCCSA (Albert Luthuli's church) encouraged non-violent opposition

Reformed Presbyterians (a black church) were slow to cohere

Quakers and Salvation Army failed to confront apartheid

Growth of Africa-initiated Churches in comparison to mainline and evangelical churches can be read as a rebuke

Hatfield Christian Church condemned both apartheid theology and liberation theology

The pattern that can be observed is that there was a gradual shift from compliance to rejection. This was more by some evangelicals than by others. However, some remained very complacent.

8.4 Sullivan Code era (1982 – 1994)

The corporate sector – not the church – introduced the Sullivan Code, in 1982. It basically told government that the economy could not grow if only whites could hold managerial and supervisory positions (that was the law at the time). There just were not enough whites to go around.

So they started admitting blacks into roles like foreman and supervisor. This opened the way for blacks to move onward and upward into management. This milestone is elaborated in Wendy Luhabe's book appropriately called <u>Defining Moments</u>.

Another crack in the walls appeared in 1986, when mixed marriages were un-banned.

The contrasts in the previous table are once again evident in this second table, but one can note a gradual sense of change.

1984 Presbyterian Church of SA (white and conservative) rejected union with the UCCSA (black majority church)

PCSA proposed sending chaplains to banned organizations

1985 Botha's visit to Moria

Institute of Contextual Theology releases its Kairos Document (see next section)

DRC releases its Church and Society document

1986 Concerned Evangelicals launched its manifesto. (It critiqued Rhema Church for flying the USA flag and for denouncing strikers.)

1987 WCC conference in Ottawa, Canada confronts the DRC: apartheid is a heresy

Split of Baptist Convention (blacks) and Baptist Union (whites)

1989 Relevant Pentecostal Witness is launched: "the colour line was washed away in the blood of the Lamb"

1990 Council of Rustenburg was attended by 97 church denominations. The theme was "repentance and restitution"

1992 IFCC (Pentecostals) joined the SACC as an "observer"

During this period, Desmond Tutu was the general secretary of the SACC. He was authorized to speak on the church's behalf without consulting member organizations first. Clearly there was momentum for change, supported by the church. But there was still a lot of scepticism and inertia as well. AFM later confessed that many of its church members held high posts in the apartheid government.

"Everything that is now covered will be uncovered, and everything now hidden will be made clear. For this reason, whatever you have said in the dark will be heard in the daylight. And what you have whispered in hidden places will be proclaimed on the housetops." (Luke 12: 2-3)

8.5 The Kairos Document

The <u>Kairos Document</u> emerged from the Institute for Contextual Theology (ICT) on September 25th, 1985. According to Willem Saayman in <u>Christian Mission in South Africa</u>:

"It elicited overwhelming reaction both inside and outside South Africa as a timely word of prophecy in the contemporary situation. It was of course also condemned by government and conservative Christians as a call to violence and labelled a Marxist, not a Christian document..." (p 88)

"I would indeed agree that Kairos has a strong evangelistic appeal. This is so because Kairos calls its readers to 'a conversion which is demanded by the serious socio-political situation in South Africa'. This call to conversion is directed at the <u>church</u>, because 'the responses of the church thus far have been totally inadequate'. This call can be compared to the call by the Old Testament prophets for the ongoing conversion of the people of God..." (p 90)

"With the Kairos Document, Christian history in South Africa can be said to have come full circle since the time of its introduction in the era of colonialism. For in its rejection of the god of State Theology, a god who legitimizes oppressive power, in Green's words (1986:52) the god who is 'a cosmic projection of colonial will, the deification of white settler power', it finally rejects the entanglement between mission and colonialism in South Africa." (p 91)

There was more than one version of the <u>Kairos Document</u> as it entered public debate. Similarly, there are different dates when different institutions declared apartheid to be a heresy – notably the Dutch Reformed denominations, the South Africa Council of Churches, and the World Council of Churches. But these were mainly in the late 1980, paving the way for the rapid changes that took place...

liberation of the captives... drafting a Constitution... free and democratic elections...

My point is that the process began at **the deepest level** of convincing devout God-fearing tax-paying citizens that they were actually worshipping an idol, not God. That done, getting the practical changes through was relatively easy.

8.6 Transition to Democracy (1994 – 2008)

During this period of rapid change, once can see the long-anticipated results unfolding:

- Rainbow nation of the children of God
- Death sentence was abolished in 1995
- Abortion on demand started in 1996
- Religious pluralism (guaranteed by the Constitution in 1997)
- Homosexuality and same-sex marriage (Civil Unions Act 2006)
- Land claims (those who has lost their land in living memory)

The evangelical response is once again captured in a table:

1994	Two Christian political parties won seats in Parliament – ACDP and UCDP
1995	TEASA confessed its "failure to develop a theology that took adequate stock of social reality"
1997	Desmond Tutu appointed to lead the Truth and Reconciliation Commission

Some new issues appeared (or re-appeared) on the agenda, like:

- Child-headed households
- Pornography
- Environmental degradation (e.g. abandoned mines that were not properly closed over)
- Corruption and patronage (e.g. the Seriti Commission)
- Abortion
- HIV policy debates (e.g. criminalization of HIV

transmission)
- Death penalty
- Intolerance
- Affirmative action

But churches have remained for the most part racially divided - led by the desire that people have to worship in their own language.

8.7 Consolidation of Democracy (2009 – 2019)

The past decade has tested both Democracy and the church's inclination to hold leaders accountable. The terms most often used are "Triumphalism" and "Impunity". The current issues requiring the church to speak truth to power are:

- Rule of Law (crime, corruption, patronage)
- Death penalty
- Malfeasance (waste, state capture)
- Gender-based violence and child protection
- Rogue pastors (i.e. wolves in sheep's clothing)
- Environmental degradation (pollution, acid rain)
- Cultural practices (e.g. virginity testing and *ukuthwala*)
- Intolerance has re-grouped under Xenophobia more than Racism
- Foundation education in the vernacular
- LAND REFORM (due to poverty, unemployment and inequality) and LAND INVASIONS
- Renewable energy (i.e. delaying Nuclear)
- Statues
- Free tertiary education (i.e. #fees must fall)
- Decriminalization of prostitution

The prophetic vocation has been exercised well by some churches:

- It was Father Stanislaus Mayibe of the Catholic Commission of Justice and Peace who filed the complaint with Public Protector Thuli Madonsela, triggering her <u>State of Capture</u> report
- The Methodist church's *Unburdening Panel* added significant

value to awareness-raising about State Capture

The church should not back off just because of the existence of
Parliament, its oversight committees, the Loyal Opposition, the
Section 9 institutions, the Judiciary, judicial commissions, ANC
sub-structures like the Integrity Commission and the Stalwarts, along
with civil society organizations and the media.

The church is still near and dear to the people, and it still has a
prophetic vocation.

For example, with respect to the prevailing methodology being
used at community level. Service delivery protests or "Violent
Democracy" often get out of hand. The church has a role to play in
peacemaking, trying to convince citizens that this is an aberration of
citizen participation.

Cultural voices are speaking out loudly. For example, the Zulu king
has banned Lobola because it was too often hi-jacked by gangsters, and
he has called for the castration of rapists.

Here are some excuses that I have heard:

- I vote for the ACDP, let them represent Christian values in
  the corridors of power
- It's no use, South Africa is too far gone to try to bring it back
  from the brink
- I keep praying for/about current events, but I am not an
  activist
- I am too busy at work, but I support my church with tithing
  and regular attendance
- The Brits had 40 years after the Anglo-Boer War, then the
  Afrikaners had their turn for 40 years under apartheid – now
  it's "their" turn. "They" won't change before "they" have had
  their 40 years of plundering the public purse

1. Communicating the Prophetic Message

First, a distinction needs to be made between a spokesperson who represents a church organization (like Pastor Ray McCauley of Rhema Church, who often writes articles for the media), and Christian individuals. When you see people from your church marching for Justice or marching for Jesus, they are "taking it personally" – not on behalf of your church. The same applies to signing Petitions and so forth. Both levels of engagement are important.

There are many media that can be used:

9.1 Sermons and motivational speaking

Pastors should address the topic of Justice on a regular basis. Keynote speakers can also be prophetic.

9.2 Print-media columns

With the rise of the Internet, print-media journals are under pressure. But they still have a place. Good writers of opinion and editorial are always welcome in the "Commentariat".

9.3 Radio and TV

Especially talk shows are a natural place for prophetic views to be voiced.

9.4 Blogsites and books

Some authors have their origins in blogging. The book trade can always find space for new writers, including poets, although it tends to keep to the authors that it already knows.

9.5 Social media

There are many options on the Internet to speak, but it is usually to peers, not to "power".

9.6 Drama and film

Theatre arts communicate complex issues well.

9.7 The Arts

Often paintings or song-writing (e.g. protest songs) can shed light on public issues.

Here is an example that is on the same theme as this book, by Hugh Wetmore, former director of the Evangelical Fellowship of South Africa:

Metre: 8787D
Tunes: Ode to Joy (Joyful, joyful we adore Thee) CD 10.13
Austria (Glorious things ...) CD 9.14
Jesus, Lord of human history,
Open wide this New Year's door;
Lead us into future's mystery
As you led your Church before.
Christ, the Alpha and Omega,
Lord of time, eternity,
God unchanging, ever eager,
Leading on to what must be.
Jesus, man of human sorrows,
You have passed through death's dark hour.
Give us hope for our tomorrows
By your resurrection power.
Give us cause for celebrations:
Bring the Year of Jubilee!
Show compassion to the nations,
Break the chains of poverty.
Jesus, crux of human choices,
Urging multitudes to say,
From among religions' voices
That you are the only Way.
Nations lose their moral bearing,

There is no integrity;
May we all, with love and daring,
Live the Truth that sets us free.
Jesus, goal of human story,
Focus of the Father's plans,
When You are revealed in glory
And the world before you stands
Then in greater celebration
All the universe will sing:
"You are head of all creation,
Sovereign Lord, Almighty King!"

This hymn was chosen for publication as one of the 44 songs (out of over 400) in the 'St Pauls Cathedral Millennium Hymn Competition' 1999. (Publication subsequently cancelled for copyright reasons.)

This Millennium Hymn was sung throughout South Africa in Richard Cock's "Songs of Praise" participatory concerts in 2000. Listen to it on CD ~ SARCD 074 (SAfm, SAMRO and Sarepta)

Church leaders need to identify and encourage lay people who can contribute regularly and meaningfully to public dialogue.

9.8 Marches

Sometimes called "demonstrations" these vary from church members picketing on the street in from of pornography shops, to inter-church events like the March for Jesus.

LA Kaufman has published a book called *How to Read a Protest: the Art of Organising and Resistance*[1]. Order it at your bookstore. Or you can rather go to Amazon and buy another book by Stephanie Hessel called *Time for Outrage!*[2] (This is the English translation of the bestselling tract *Indignez-vous!* by the French diplomat, member of the French Resistance and concentration camp survivor Stéphane Hessel).

---

1.   *https://www.ucpress.edu/book/9780520301528/how-to-read-a-protest*

2.   *https://www.amazon.com/Time-Outrage-Indignez-vous-St%C3%A9phane-Hessel/dp/
      1455509728*

9.9 Petitions

Getting signatures on petitions has become quite commonplace. Combined with social media, it can obtain huge numbers of signatories on its petitions.

9.10 Academic research

In the spheres of law, sociology, philosophy and theology, there is room for relevant debate. Paul Freston's book <u>Evangelicals and Politics in Asia, Africa and Latin America</u> is a good example.

9.11 Memorials

These could vary from memorial lectures (one is proposed for the activist Andies Tatane) to calendars celebrating activism to stained-glass windows in churches.

9.12 Civil Disobedience

Non-violence is a prerequisite. Back in the days of apartheid, some Christians refused to go to war. They asked to be deployed in community service instead. Some ended up in jail, but in the later years of apartheid, conscientious objection was recognized for what it is.

When you are participating in a protest, and the authorities say, "You can march, but you cannot wear masks", it is human nature to call their bluff. Our advice is to march without a mask. Just as you can agree to disagree, you can also be obedient in your disrespect.

In closing, I cannot let Prayer go un-mentioned. But I am not creating another section (9.13) because this is cross-cutting. All of the above interventions should include a measure of prayer. Prayer is not really a "social" media – unless by "social" you mean that you are talking to the Trinity (God in three persons)! But prayer is certainly communicating our message, and it is just as important that we communicate our concerns to heaven as on earth. After all, we were taught to pray:

Thy will be done
On earth as it is in heaven

In his book Those Who Show Up, Andy Flannagan offers a great example of including prayer in activities:

"This year has also seen the launching of Restore groups around the UK. They are based on asking a very simple, question, 'What would a restored version of our community look like?' Groups brainstorm this question for twenty minutes, pray for twenty minutes, then plot and scheme for twenty minutes. Some of the answers lead to practical direct action, but many of the conclusions drawn by groups are that they need to be in positions of influence in their local communities to see the sort of transformation they desire taking place...

Prayer is not more important, or less important. It is integral.

"We are not trying to say that politics is more important than, say, prayer, or direct action, in any given community, but that at the moment, there are far less of us doing politics, compared to the other two. Could we be part of that changing? It is important however not to be lulled into a utilitarian gospel that is all about sorting out the world. Public leadership transcends just 'sorting things out'. Leadership in the public square does shape culture for better or for worse, either creating or shutting down the space for certain strands of thought and action. It is an influence on the personal and spiritual realm too. When we abdicate ourselves from that sort of leadership we allow those who would wish to operate from a utilitarian mindset to dominate the imaginations of people. We will be left with no defence against the de facto definition of humans as economic units and the ensuing exploitation, consumerism and individualism.

In Romans chapter 12, St Paul says that we should be "continuing instant in prayer". The motto of the monasteries captured this: *Ora et labora*. Pray and work.

Pray for personal renewal as well as social renewal. Redemption is not just for individual souls, but for communities, cultures and societies as well. And even for our planet.

Did you love *Let Justice Roll On Like a River*? Then you should read *Opa Waxes Prophetic*[1] by CO Stephens!

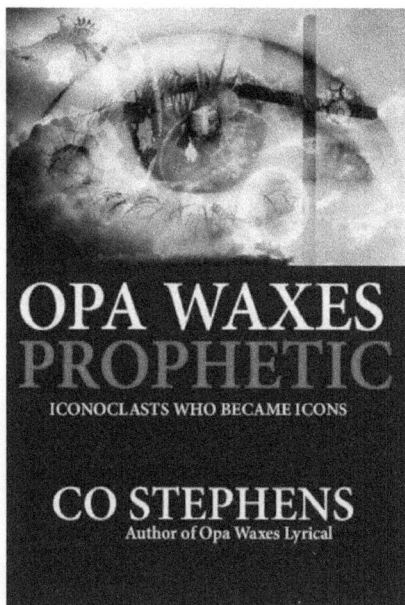

This book is about "speaking truth to power." It contains word-pictures of dozens of iconoclasts who (ironically) themselves became icons. But they inspire us to keep up the momentum of change. However, the author does set outer limits, because change has often taken history to places where it shouldn't go. The book is predicated on an understanding that Prophecy is less about foresight, and more about insight. "The words of the prophets are written on the subway walls... in tenement halls..." indeed. Change is interruptive by nature and change agents are always provocative.

---

1. https://books2read.com/u/mVKVjJ

2. https://books2read.com/u/mVKVjJ

Also by Mbokodo Publishers

Let Justice Roll On Like a River

Also by CO Stephens

Opa Waxes Prophetic
Orania and Azania
Rich Man, Poor Woman, Bogyman, Thief
Let Justice Roll On Like a River

About the Publisher

Mbokodo Publishers is your choice service provider and partner in the publishing business. We make your business our business in order to understand your needs, tastes and challenges better so we could provide you with the most efficient services imaginable.

Our professional and committed staff and personnel are always ready to assist you whenever you contact us. So drop us an email or simply call or visit our offices and this could be the beginning of a positive change in your life!

We look forward to being of ultimate assistance to you our dear prospective clients. For more information with regards to our offered products and services, please email us, mbokodopublishers@gmail.com

We look forward to hearing from you soon. God bless you!

Regards,

Publisher

www.ingramcontent.com/pod-product-compliance
Lightning Source LLC
La Vergne TN
LVHW091313080426
835510LV00007B/484